ISBN 978-1-332-17530-7
PIBN 10293976

English
Français
Deutsche
Italiano
Español
Português

www.forgottenbooks.com

Mythology Photography **Fiction**
Fishing Christianity **Art** Cooking
Essays Buddhism Freemasonry
Medicine **Biology** Music **Ancient**
Egypt Evolution Carpentry Physics
Dance Geology **Mathematics** Fitness
Shakespeare **Folklore** Yoga Marketing
Confidence Immortality Biographies
Poetry **Psychology** Witchcraft
Electronics Chemistry History **Law**
Accounting **Philosophy** Anthropology
Alchemy Drama Quantum Mechanics
Atheism Sexual Health **Ancient History**
Entrepreneurship Languages Sport
Paleontology Needlework Islam
Metaphysics Investment Archaeology
Parenting Statistics Criminology
Motivational

A Panoramic View

OF THE

CREATION!

IN THE

Light of Geology.

BY MRS. ROZINA GATES,

Bangor, Van Buren Co., Mich.

————•————

————

ST. JOSEPH, MICH. :
THEO. L. REYNOLDS, PRINTER.
1871.

A PANORAMIC VIEW

OF THE

CREATION,

IN THE LIGHT OF GEOLOGY.

By Mrs. Rozina Gates.

——:o:——

The great Sahara Desert wild
Was once the ocean bed,
And the oasis smiling now
In time will o'er it spread.

Yes, where are now those sandy plains
Once roll'd the foaming tide,
But the eruptions of the earth
Forc'd it on another side.

Your earth, it widely ope'd its mouth,
And clos'd above the tide,
But on the bosom of the same,
Your gallant ships do ride.

We write from France and Italy,
Places of renown,
And what we know of interest
Endeavor to pen down.

Some may deride our history
And call it all a hoax,
But the oasis smiling now
Once issued fire and smoke.

In time a river smooth and deep
Will be flowing o'er those sands,
Where now is but a waste so wild
There liveth not a man.

And there the white-winged messenger
Will be sailing o'er its tide ;
You may sneer at our poetry,
And you may it deride.

Those waters there will intersect
The Atlantic and Red Sea,
And what compose Niagara Falls
In time will break-away.

Some cities then will be ruined quite,
For their larks will loose their wings ;
They cannot sail as they do now,
Another song they'll sing.

Then you cannot do as you have done,
Ship your freight across,
And necessitated you will be,
To drive the iron horse.

And where are now your pleasant lakes,
Will be valleys of dry land;
We mean the upper and lower ones,
That bound State Michigan.

And where also is your Erie Lake,
A valley you will see,
When that mighty cataract
Ceases such to be.

The same grand power that form'd it there
Will it in sunder break _
The waters of those lakes gushed forth,
When your earth mightily quaked.

A mighty earth-quake did pass through,
In terrific waves ;
Forming the basins of those lakes
Where the fishes now do lave.

But Oh, the doleful news will ring,
Will ring from shore to shore,
When that mighty cataract
Is cataract no more.

'Twill sweep its thousands with the flood,
Of brute and human too,
But your earth will still keep moving on
As they to the ocean go.

'Twill sweep off mills and houses too,
With all the goods they own,
Leaving whole families in woe
In their distress to mourn.

But your earth will still keep moving on,
In its yearly round,
Until Christs's Kingdom it shall come,
And this be hallowed ground.

You look for the Millenial morn,
But your earth, so fair and grand,
Will never be consumed by fire.
As you may understand.

Sure it will never be destroyed,
As you've been taught no, no,
But the electric fires of Heaven
Throughout your earth must glow.

Then your prison doors will loose their bolts,
And not be needed there,
And orphan children find a home,
And have a mother's care.

Then plow-shares will be made of swords,
And pruning-hooks of spears ;
And the nations will learn war no more,
Throughout your earthly sphere.

Then Jews and Gentiles will not disagree,
Not disagree at all ;
But you'll have one church and government
Upon your earthly ball.

But you in a fiery chariot
To heaven will never go,-
As you read did good Elijah,
In days of long ago.

But you'll pluck the flowers from life's fair tree,
That bloom in Heavenly spheres ;
And the angels that have past away
Will pluck your flowers here.

Then death in time will loose its sting,
And the grave its victory too,
When men and angels hand in hand,
Throughout life's sphere shall go.

Then the beauties of the spirit land
So resplendant will appear,
That when your friends they pass away,
·You will not shed a tear.

But when you shroud the cold dead form,
And fit it for the tomb, ·
You'll feel like dressing up a bride ,
And presenting to the groom.

But the valleys of your pleasant lakes,
Will be valleys of rich earth,
Where teeming millions in future time
Will have a perfect birth.

There grass will grow and waving grain,
With fruits and flowers so fair ;
And the angelic choristers
With music fill the air.

But where are now your prairies wide
Was once the raging flood;
Remember this is possible :
Behold you have a God!

But some would ask where are the banks
Which this a basin made,
They have blown off in particles,
By winds they call the trade.

First the ocean then the forest wild,
And then it was submerg'd ;
But since became the prairies wide,
And there the lowing herds·

But on those prairies vast and wide
In some places that are dry,
With springs and brooks and larger streams,
Will those places be supplied,

And where water now surrounds the poles,
In time there will be land ;
Your earth has changes very great
We'd have you understand.

For it throws off and it takes on,
As it journeys round the sun ;
Differing far from what it was
When it's motion first begun.

But aye or nay it took we know,
So firm the Granite Rock;
It was not into being spoke ;
At one single shock.

And there are deserts loan and drear,
Where will be trees, shrubs and plants;
With fruits and flowers of various hues,
And there sparkling streams will dance.

You may wonder sure, how they can have
Streams, trees, shrubs, and plants,
They'll be form'd by that intrinsic essence
Which some would term by chance.

The Poles of earth, they long are bound
In an icy chain ;
But they'll have more congenial suns,
And assume another name.

And new continents they will come forth
From beneath the ocean bed,
And where surging billows now do play,
Will vegetation spread.

Your earth convulses day by day,
And hour by hour likewise;
And in this way Islands are form'd,
And new continents arise.

Islands and continents have rose and fell,
Since your earth revolved around;
And there was land once to be seen,
Where is now Long Island Sound.

A continent did once exist,
Having climate fair and mild,
But a share sunk 'neath the briny deep,
Forming the Friendly Isles.

And where also are some great ravines,
Once mov'd the curling foam,
Dashing, splashing on the beach,
The waves were hurried on.

But some would ask, where are they now,
Or have their waters dried,
They have retired to their sister floods,
Through deep tunnels under-side.

And the eruptions of the earth
Have closed the tunnel's mouths.
The truth of our assertions here,
Some perhaps may doubt.

There's much that's back, far back we know,
Which a mystery would seem,
And many educated men
Have never of it dreamed.

For whole nations have been swallow'd up,
In the bowels of the earth,
Who, in strength and size did far exceed
Some which since have had a birth.

And traces of them have been found.
And implements they used,
But loves and laws of those nations, they,
Often did abuse.

Your now call'd Salt Lake City
Will be engulf'd in wave ;
Not all the salt that's in that Lake,
Could n'er the city save.

For a mighty water-spout will ope,
And engulf it all in wave,
So all the salt that's in that Lake
Could n'er the city save.

A tunnel it is making through,
To that briny Lake;
And all who would their lives preserve,
The city should forsake.

And your Pacific iron road.
Must take another route,
For it will be engulf'd in wave,
By this great water-spout.

Some valleys will be filled with wave,
You may think we'er talking tall,
The waters they are changing more,
Upon your earthly ball.

And some passes in your mountains,
Will be straits yet in the sea,
With mighty promontories,
It's truth we'er telling thee.

Your earth moves in an orbit round,
And changes there must be,
From land to sea, and sea to land,
To make all things agree.

But the beauties of those high lands
With their trees of evergreen,
In no other region,
We think could e'er be seen.

And your now call'd Lake Ontario.
And Lake Baikal too, beside,
The time will come when you will learn
Their basins will be dry.

Our statements are no miracles,
But with nature do accord ;
There never was a miracle,
Since roll'd your mighty Orb.

But the waters of Ontario,
Are sinking many know,
And your pleasant Ridge-road,
Was it's beach, yes long ago.

But between this Lake and ridge there are
Trees of the tallest kind,
Which seem to bow in reverence,
To Him who is Divine.

And there are lakes which are called seas,
With no outlet plain in view ;
But they have outlets underneath,
Where the water gushes through.

Tornadoes wild, and hurricanes,
More frequent will appear,
On your western Continent,
In the northern hemisphere.

Tornadoes wild, and hurricanes,
Strewing wrecks on sea and land :
Their origin perhaps, you all
Do not quite understand.

It's the electric combined powers,
Both in the earth and out,
And when they burst up through the sea
Produce great water-spouts.

But when the power loses its force,
And the tunnel it is cool,
Then the waters they go rushing through,
And it becomes a pool.

The whirlpools in the ocean wide,
Are heads of mighty streams,
On which do play your gallant ships,
As they rush back to the Main.

The ocean bed has tunnels deep,
Through which their waters glide,
And they gush forth in springs and streams,
Fresh on the other side.

But where the distance is but short
From ocean bed to fount,
You'll find their waters pure and bright,
And there the speckled Trout.

In mineral waters they could not live,
Nor in a mudy stream ;
But in waters pure and bright,
Will the speckled Trout be seen.

Seas interspersed with many isles,
Called archipelagoes ;
By the eruptions of the earth
They have been formed we know.

Your earth had once a smoother face,
But some would this deride ;
The internal fires in their passage through,
Have thrown up its rocky sides.

And on their passage lit the wood,
And consumed it into coal ;
With a mighty thundering voice,
As they through earth have roll'd,

A mighty earthquake will pass through
Near the rocky range,
And the rich jewels of the earth
Become molten veins.

Your earth has many veins of gold,
Once mixed with earth and sand,
Congealed by the internal fires,
Now please to understand.

And visionary minds, they will
Discover it in part;
Your earth is turning inside out,
Time will expose its heart.

Rich veins of gold lie hid all through,
In climates warm and cold,
In time like lilly buds, they will
Their golden leaves unfold.

Its growing now like quarry stones,
Or coal that lies in beds;
You may wonder at our novelty,
They're nourished by the dead.

Your earth increases in its size.
Taking a larger belt,
And we will venture for to say,
Hath lungs and heart and milt.

It is composed of webs or strings
In its very depths,
Being a substance tangible,
Which spirit hands have felt.

If they could penetrate thick walls
And your panes of glass,
Into the bowels of earth,
They likewise could pass.

This substance is the spine of earth,
Serving as electric wires
With here and there a switch also,
Where pass the electric fires.

Likewise a safeguard sure it hath,
Running from pole to pole,
Serving to keep it in its place :
In its orbit where it rolls.

And the life-tide of your rolling orb,
Changes continually ;
. Passing through its very heart, .
Causing the ebb and flow.

It changes, yes, continually,
Like the tide of human forms ; .
Perhaps some would debate with us,
But we must march along.

We will not stop for wind or wave,
We know 'twill never do ;
We've started on our journey straight,
And we must travel through,

It's not composed of miles or leagues,
No distance here we trace ;
Our journey is of charity,
We're a christian race.

We must describe more minutely
Your mighty rolling orb,
Which has nerves and sinews too,
Nature with it accords.

The waters flow through it's heart and veins,
As we have here described ;
Though at times appear quite motionless,
And calmly seem to lie.

And your mighty globe has a shell or crust,
Which we will term it's hide,
And the internal fires have
Thrown up its rocky sides.

And it often has convulsions
Which burst out in the sea,
On your western continent,
Near South America.

And whole countries in that region,
Will be engulf'd in wave,
The fires are nearing now it's coast,
And nothing will it save.

And all along the Pacific line
Will be tumultuous waves,
Caused by eruptions of the earth,
Appalling hearts so brave.

And the ocean bed will be thrown up
Near San Francisco Bay,
Devastating the country round,
And it in ruins lay.

It must needs be, that earth's fires roll,
To keep it moving on ;
This is no judgment or miracle,
We tell you in our song.

Your earth it is a mighty globe,
Formed by a mighty power ;
But nature shows it ne'er was formed,
In six times four and twenty hours.

You read 'twas without form and void,
And darkness was on the deep ;
When suddenly God made one man,
And put him fast to sleep.

But this is a progressive world,
Fast moves this rolling ear ;
Lighted all o'er by the sun and moon,
And little blazing stars.

But it has changes, changes sure,
And some in meter we will tell,
For there was land once to be seen,
Where the mighty waves now swell.

On the eastern coast of America,
Earth's fiercest fires have rolled,
And the flinty rocks raised from their beds,
But this was done of old.

And some are robed in moss and vines,
And trees fair to be seen,
Which bow their lovely, gentle heads,
And they're called evergreen.

Those rocks were formed of clay and sand,
And a mixture of the brine ;   [was,
But they were not formed as you read the earth
In six days of time.

Your earth it was quite small indeed,
When its motion first begun,
Imparting less than it took on,
As it journeyed round the sun.

We do admit your past off sires,
Sends intellectual rays,
Which will be as mighty meteors
Causing a perfect day.

If the waters of your globe were still,
All living there would die ;
They must have air and motion too,
To keep them all alive.

You earth has lungs, please understand :
Through which do fly its fires ;
And it all through has passages,
Electric as your wires.

In Missouri's tributaries,
Way up in Montana ;
If you turn their streams, you'll find the ore,
Deep bedded there it lies.

Rich veins of gold lie hid all through,
Covered by mother earth ;
Which time and nature must unface,
To the filling of your purse,

God made the earth ! He made the gold,
And He made you and me ;
And He made the fishes, great and small,
That are swimming in the sea.

But He did not make them all at once,
There's no such thing, we know ;
And from the very elements,
Fishes and man did grow.

You may strain the waters of the sea,
And put in gravel pans ;
Soon the fishes will be sailing round,
Oh, test us if you can.

The very air, the breath you breath,
Is origin of life ;
Oh, you may with us debate.
You have no chance for strife,

And new species are developed,
Upon your earthly shore ;
Behold ! it is not finished quite,
'Twill take some six days more.

Your earth has changes, vast and great,
On its kingdoms we do know ,
And your now-called Snake-head Indians
Once had neither foot nor toe.

But crept among the grass and ferns,
Like the reptile on the plain ;
Although he has progressed we know,
The snake shows on the brain.

Man's origin is not understood
At the present day ;
Although your Bible plainly tells,
That he was made of clay.

Man has come forth from animal,
Crawling much like the the snail ;
Progressing as the pollywog.
Which in the water sails.

And so on up to higher life,
'Till he became a man ;
What think you of this clay one,
Oh tell me if you can.

Man once had hair, much like the beast,
And on all fours he crept,
The truthfulness of our history,
All may not accept.

He once did creep, he once did hop,
Then a species of the frog;
But changed from that development,
To a species of the dog.

And he changes every seven years,
So three times twenty-one,
And thus keeps changing on
'Till life with him done.

But next to man in intellect,
Is the dog we very well know;
And through various forms of development,
Man has come up also.

But he was of vegetation formed,
Before he crept on earth,
And now he is of human,
And has a spirit birth.

You read all things are possible
With Him who rules on high;
And from the loliest creeping thing
Comes forth the butterfly.

But man to God is near allied
God of the Universe.
But when he lays the mortal by
His spirit comes to earth.

But he progresses on and on,
And has, since life with him began ;
Before and since he stood erect
Or call'd himself a man.

But he once in the ocean stood
With a flower on his head,
And now he is intelligent
And earns his daily bread.

But when he lays the mortal off
And puts the immortal on,
With him there is a greater change
Than we speak of in our song.

Yes, when his spirit soars away
And his form in the coffin laid,
With him there is a greater change
Than e'er before was made.

Just think of this ! the spirit lives
While the body it is dead,
Being developed from a lovely stalk,
With a flower on its head.

And well may man say mother earth,
When he forth from it came,
Like the blooming flower in early spring,
Not bearing his present name.

We're reminded of the poet, sure,
For truly hath he said :
Life's a vapor, man's a flower,
For it was upon his head.

That flower was called sweet Bethlehem,
Which in the ocean grew,
And the angels bright, receiving light,
Are giving it to you.

We hope to tell you all about
Old Adam and his wife,
And should you dare us to oppose,
We'll comely meet the strife.

You think that God a spirit is,
But what in ancient day,
He the breath of life in the nostrils breathed,
Of the man He'd made of clay.

If this was God, He's changed his sphere,
Likewise, He's changed His mode ;
You read He is not changeable.
Your Father and your God.

We do expect to sow some seed
That will fall upon good ground ;
And the angels, from their spheres above,
Will harrow it around.

And it must spread like prairie fires,
With nothing to impede,
And we from Heaven, with manna, sure,
Will endeavor you to feed.

You've often heard, in thunder tones
Like the war-cry on the plain,
Of this horrid pit, the brimstone lake
Where thousands must remain.

Old theology, from press and desk
Preached it in lofty strains,
But the angels, from the spheres above,
Have broke its jaws in twain.

T'was more the dread of the brimstone lake
And of your Maker's ire,
Which caused many after holiness
And heaven to inquire.

But now that lake has ceased to burn,
Of brimstone and of fire ;
Some do look up, thinking their God
Is not of wrath and ire.

He is all love and goodness
That man could e're concede,
And if you wish his power to know,
In the book of nature read.

The planets that are rolling through
Immensity of space,
Of soul and body compose a part
Of Him who did create.

God is not seated on a Throne,
Apart, and high above
His earthly children on your plain,
For all of you he loves.

Behold ! His Throne is everywhere,
In heaven and earth and sea ;
In deepest caverns of your earth,
Likewise His Throne must be.

It is not fire high up in air,
As many do suppose ;
And all that's in creation's plan
His body does compose.

His spirit fills immensity,
Immensity of space ;
So God the soul and body is
Of all He does create.

Well hath this soul enlivening power
Which in Deity exists,
And all that man on earth can learn,
The spirits they can teach.

Models and drawings they can present
To some visions on your plain,
But if all for this are not organized
Do not of us complain.

We more would add to your happiness,
And we would give you light ;
Oh l heed our council ye earthly ones,
Though we are out of sight.

Man hardly knows, now, what he knows,
But guesses some, in part,
But nature, with its open book,
Will soon give him a start.

He will see God in the mirror
Plain as he can anywhere ;
In the heavens above, the earth beneath,
Of fruits and flowers so fair.

The ancients they did not believe
That the earth was round ;
And in consequence of this they thought,
Of course it would'nt drown.

They thought it flat just like a board
And on the waters moved ;
But mariners who sail'd it round,
Its rotundity have proved.

Truth crushed to earth will rise again,
No power can it destroy ;
But Geology proves your Bible
To be but a mere toy.

The Bible speaks of Noah's flood
As drowning of the world,
Which we think was impossible
As it on its axis whirled.

The Ark-was built of Gopher wood,
And on the waters it did ride,
But all that Noah left behind
The bible tells it died.

Noah had quite a family
In the Ark with him to ride,
Of toads and frogs and lizzards,
And many things beside·

He must have had the black snakes,
The hippopotamus too,
The grizzly bears and wolverines,
Likewise the buffalo.

Of course he had the rein-deers
Which are so nice to run,
The rattle-snakes, the blow-snakes,
The hoop and mocasin.

He must have had the blow-snakes
All on the leeward side.
For all who took their poison breath
We know they must have died.

Some must have crossed the ocean wide
From undiscovered isles,
Oh, he had the Bengal tigers,
Likewise the crocodile.

He had all kinds of ferocious beasts
From countries, too, afar,
But he caged them up with Gopher wood
Instead of iron bars.

He must have had, of each, a pair
From the islands of the sea,
But if all were not discovered then.
How, in reason, could it be.

We hope in time mankind will have,
On earth, good, common sense,
No matter what he reads in books,
He'll stand beside the fence.

There might have been a deluge
In a portion of the land,
But not such a mighty one
As many understand.

Look at the reason, if you will,
To think the world was drown'd.
How, in reason could it be ?
For, behold ! you know it's rouud.

Attractions, yes, of land and see,
There must be on its face,
To keep the waters where they are,
In their destined place.

Your God will ne'er destroy his works
In such a foolish way,
And if all were righteous in the ark,
Why not righteous now, to-day ?
That's the question ?

Your Bible is the best of books
'Though it some big stories tell,
But if you can't believe them, quite,
We think it's just as well.

Oh ! truly, it is like a harp,
A harp of many strings,
No matter where you touch a key
You any tune can sing.

Though it's thought to be a mighty book,
We'll have it all transposed,
And write it all in poetry,
Though it's written now in prose.

And there are contradictions
And some ideas we spurn,
For the traveler to the spirit-land
Back to earth, we know, returns.

But we think it a mere history,
A history of the past,
And should you make it examplary
Into prison you'd be cast.

It has caus'd more wars and suffering
Than all other wars combin'd ;
Think of Adoniram Judson,
And Ann Hazzletine.

And those devoted Christians
Who with them sail'd away
To the land of dark Pagodas,
Where they long in prison lay·

Think of the galling fetters,
Likewise the galling chains,
With bent limbs, all cramped and crippled,
While they in prison long remain' d l

Think of the knife uplifted
To take the breath away !
Likewise the dark brow'd Burmahns,
And the tropics' sick'ning ray l

It was all for the Bible
Those little feet did trip,
And those babes pass'd on so merrily
To see the gallant ship.

Think of a mother's feelings
When that ship it left the bay,
Giving it's canvass to the breeze,
Bearing her babes away.

She wep't, she prayed,
She wrung her hands,
You may imagine how,   [now.
Saying : so dear a sacrifice I never made ?'till

And think, too, of the martyrs
Who by thousands have been slain ;
But on your good, old Bible
Is left the bloody stain.

It calls God good, it Calls Him bad,
Yes, angry every day ;
Your Bible's like a Fiddle,
You any tune can play.

God, truly, is a God of love
And as Father we Him claim,
But, oh ! your good, old Bible
Is a libel on His name.

It calls your God a tyrant,
And likewise a fool ;
Think you, did the Bible writers
Ever go to school?

Or if they were inspired
The Bible for to write,
Then why such contradictions,
Put down in black and white ?

God. truly, is all wisdom l
He's provided everywhere
For the keeping of the Nations
Sprinkled here and there.

There is no virus in the land,
We care not where it floats,
But God, in his providence,
Has for it an antidote.

It gushes forth from mother earth,
Is found in roots and herbs,
In flowers, too, and barks of trees,
And in mineral waters stored.

But Heaven we think a dangerous place,
If Satan from it came,
Here to be bound a thousand years,
Then to be loos'd again.

But just think of the serpent
Which tempted Mother Eve,
And her eyes they being opened,
She aprons made of leaves,

For God was in the Garden,
And Eve and Adam heard Him there,
And they thought that Fig-tree aprons
Would be proper for to wear.

It seems that God was a person then,
Not present everywhere,
For He walked out in the Garden
To take the morning air.

But he form'd Adam out of dust,
And in his nostrils breath'd,
And he became a living soul,
So many do believe.

But Adam was quite lonely
While in the garden there,
So God of children bethought himself,
That he would have a pair.

And, if the Bible it be true,
Took a rib from Ádams' side,
Of which He did a Woman make
And gave her as a Bride.

Be sure it was an easy thing,
For he was put to sleep,
And we suppose he closed the wound,
And then did him awake.

God was not Omnipresent then,
Nor Omnipotent, i o, no,
He'd just commenced in the Garden
Our first parents for to grow.

They were a little family,
Having but little strife,
While Cain went off to the land of Nod
To hunt him up a wife.

God has progressed some since that time,
As we shall plainly show,
He's built a Throne for Himself on high,
And a Hell for man below.

But Hell is not feared quite as much
As it was in by-gone days,
So your paper fences have tumbled down,
And your lambs have gone away.

You thought that God did make all things,
So beautiful and grand,
And when He had made Adam and Eve,
The stars together sang.

And you think that God did make your earth,
Of rotundity so great,
And when He'd finished up his work,
Made Adam, as they state.

Your world has been in darkness
For centuries, you see,
But when the light of Heaven shines,
Then darkness it must flee.

You thought you should not love the earth
Nor anything below,
But your affections placed above,
Which Godliness would show.

Oh, you should love your earthly plain,
For God hath made it fair;
No matter if you worship it,
For He is everywhere.

And if you love your Maker, God,
You love everything you see;
For He pervades matter and space,
Then everywhere must be.

Sure, He is in the mountains high
And the bowels of the earth,
And every little floweret
That ever did have birth.

He's in lofty trees that wave
And in grains of sand,
And he formed the models of your ships
Which sail at your command.

They, truly, had their origin
In spirit, in Deity,
The models of your mighty ships
Which are sailing far at sea.

If God could form your earthly ball
And roll it high in space,
Then he could plan your ships at sea,
To carry round your freight.

Some think God deficient in
Things of a simple kind,
But think he made the sun and moon
And little stars that shine.

He made all that is beautiful,
Made everything you see,
But do you think the Ark contained
All living, as they say.

We do not wish to censure
That gracious, good, old book,
They wrote as they did understand,
Or so to us it looks.

But man, he surely has progress'd
In eighteen hundred years,
If, truly, this were not the case,
We think it would be queer.

Some think that God is afar off,
But once He was so near
He made one man, Adam, of clay,
And a woman made so queer.

And another time he was so near
He was heard by this young pair,
As He in the garden walked
To take the cooling air.

It seems the serpent did a feat
Which a blessing is to all,
He ope'd the eyes of this young pair
Or you could not see at all.

And you, surely, should show him respect
For this blessing on your race;
If the serpent had not ope'd their eyes
You'd all been blind to-day.

So good, you see, through evil comes,
Or proved so, in this case,
And Adam's sin, a blessing is
To all his sinful race.

The generations weaker grew
And wiser, so they say,
If you do not understand the phrase
We'll explain it, by the way.

They weaker grew in faith which they
Have had in by-gone days,
They know a living Father rules
O'er heaven and earth and sea.

They have been taught, an angry God
Was their Heavenly Father, sure,
And that the anger of his wrath
They, forever, must endure.

But they became more wise, now, still,
Since angels came to earth,
Concerning Christ, the principle,
Which knew no death or birth.

They learn that Jesus was a man
And earthly parents had,
But the Christ principle was with
The, so called, Son of God.

This principle was before the world
Had its foundation laid,
But eighteen hundred years ago
Some, of it, were afraid.

Some were afraid the world would be
Filled with this light, Divine,
But man, he was progressing, sure,
Before he counted time.

But he progresses faster now
Than he did in days of yore,
For he has teachers from on high,
Who scan creation o'er.

But now they come, as teachers true,
On your plain below,
And them, no earthly powers can
Their teachings overthrow.

For nature, yes, and nature's God,
Show their teachings to be true,
Corroberating with it all,
The old as well as new.

Old age and illness they come on.
As you are well aware,
But the sooner in the spirit-land
It's blessings you will share.

Your earth, it undergoes a change
In one eternal round,
And what is plenty in your sphere,
In time it can't be-found.

The fruits and flowers that now you have
In your zones so mild,
In time they will desert you here
And on other climes they'll smile.

You know that prophets were to come
In these later days,
Now try to test them, if you can,
Remember what they say.

They'll turn your earth all upside down,
To use a common phrase,
But He that rolls it in its orb
Perhaps, can keep it straight.

In time, the bowels of your earth
Will turn inside out,
What think you, skeptics, now, of this ?
Oh ! you may have your doubts.

You once did doubt the earth was round
And in an orbit roll'd,
Remember God the ruler, high,
He doth all things controll.

And if He could make such a ball
And roll it high in air,
Then he could turn it inside out,
It's true, we do declare !

The internal fires that now do burn
In the bowels of your earth,
Serve as steam to the iron horse,
Driving the engine forth.

They serve to turn your earthly ball
And keep it in its place,
In it's orbit where it moves,
Rolling high in space.

When thousands of years have rolled away,
Mankind will surely see,
The torrid will be frigid then,
And the frigid torrid be.

But away, among the rocky heights,
Where gold mining is begun,
You'll go in mighty companies
And gather by the ton.

The ore, we mean, the shining ore,
The gold-God of the earth,
The God whom many worship,
The gold-God of the earth.

But where there are no waving trees,
Though I tell it now in rhyme,
You'll plant as mighty orchards,
The maple and the pine.

For sawing and for wood-lands,
And for sugar-making, too,
And learn to make an eden
Where is but desert now.

You'll set thick hedges round your fields
Of fruit and grain and grass,
Then thickly set the evergreens
To protect from chilling blasts.

You'll plant your seeds from grafted fruit,
Then let them natural grow,
You'll learn they'll better stand the winds
Which o'er the prairies blow.

You every day learn something new
If angels do you teach,
And what you call your gospel now
You'll be ashamed to teach.

The wisest lived in olden time,
Pray do not at us rail,
You can't compete with their fishing, no,
Neither their catching quails.

The quails that fell around the camp,
Camp of the Israelites,
If you should see them all compact
Oh, they might you affright.

They'd make a wall around your earth
Equal to the Chinese,
Sufficient, yes, in thickness for
Several to ride abreast.

The mountains you volcanoes call,
Were seen of ancient date,
And thought to be the mighty mouths
Of the burning brimstone lake.

But we think that it has ceased to burn,
For we hear not of late
From press or desk, of this horrid pit,
The burning, brimstone lake.

Some mothers, dear, have wept aloud
When their children have cross'd o'er,
Thinking the torments of this lake
They'd endure forever-more.

But now they come, like Noah's Dove
Who left the Ark unfold,
And to this dark, benighted land
They many truths have told.

We shall reveal so much to you
Your Convents they will ope',
Breaking the shackles of the Romish Church
With curses to the Pope.

Your Government it is all base,
Imperfect, mean, and low,
But we, from Heaven's Eternal Throne,
A perfect one will show.

We'll raise a flag that sure must flaunt
In yon blue ether air,
And the Nations all for it will shout,
So never more dispair.

We've watched the rolling of your sphere,
For centuries gone by,
And those who've past to higher life,
Against you they do cry.

We want your world for to progress
Faster than it does now,
And if you with our counsel heed
We'll try to tell you how.

Now if you wish for to progress
We'll tell you what to do,
Just keep the angels paramount
And crush the brute below.

All try for to confine yourselves
To what is just and good,
And then your sight will be so clear
You'll see beyond the flood.

Then you'll attract the angels bright
To such a high degree,
That when mankind steps on earth's plane
Better organized they'll be.

Then you'll progress to higher life,
Higher and still higher,
Until the animal in man
There wholly does expire.

And then you'll see Christ's Kingdom come,
But not Jesus in the air
As many christians they have thought,
You ne'er will see him there.

But you will see peace on your earth,
And an exercised good will,
And as the waters cover the earth
It with righteous will be fill'd

Then you'd learn to live with labor less,
But our idea never scorn,
You'll be busy as the little bee
Which blows his tiny horn.

You'll study arts and sciences,
All the mind could ever scan,
Likewise the highest interests
Of the god-part of man.

You're in your Alphabet to-day
Concerning spirit life,
And the very lines we here do pen
They will create a strife.

Some will think it's all the Medium
That we are writing through,
For their visions are too limited
To understand it now.

But such can feed on milk a while,
If they're to weak for meat;
If they can't understand us quite,
When we attempt to speak.

When a few more revolutions,
Your earth makes round the sun,
Perhaps you'll better understand
Us spirits when we come.

For soon you'll see, yes eye to eye,
And face to face we say;
All things will be transform'd anew,
And the old be done away.

Then your paper fences will tumble down,
And Christ will be the wall
Which will surround the church of God,
This is the one and all.

There will be no bigots in his church,
Nor sectarians, no, no ;
But peace from Heaven, like a mighty stream
Throughout your earth must flow.

Some think the world it retrogrades,
But it's nonsense thus to speak ;
And those who think this is the case,
Their minds they must be weak.

But everything it must progress,
In heaven, and earth, and sea ;
Animals, birds, and fishes all,
Mankind and Deity.

But this may seem quite novel sure,
To think God does progress;
The holy, lofty and the high,
Who gives you food and rest.

He surely must progress, we know
To be ahead of man ;
Although he is the Deity,
Who does creation scan.

There's nought on earth that dormant lies,
There's no such thing we know ;
All must progress or retrograde,
As nature plainly shows.

Perhaps the motion of your earth
You all do understand ;
Knowing the power of Him who rules,
Who holds it in His hand.

Your earthly ball, a spirit hath,
As much as morta l man ;
Connected with the mighty flood,
Which serves to roll it on.

The attractions of the moon ne'er made,
The tides to ebb or flow,
For out they go, and in they come,
As the earth turns round we know.

You're taught the mountains are to melt,
And seas are to retire.
And this earthly ball on which you live,
All be consumed by fire.

But we think that God would foolish be,
To make so fair a ball,
And then turn round and burn it up.
Having no cause at all.

His works he never will consume,
He maketh no play-toys
To use a while, then tear in bits,
Like many foolish boys. :

Your earthly ball a Paradise,
Will be sure below ;
No matter what you read in books,
The angels they do know.

But you should rightly organize,
Yes, make all right the brain,
And if you step in virtues path,
Try there for to remain.

No bolts or locks you then will need,
To safely keep your doors ;
But Heaven, will its windows ope,
And its blessings on you pour.

Then wars will cease throughout your lands,
And nations no more it learn,
Your spears be used for pruning-hooks,
And your swords to plow-shares turn.

We do expect to war awhile.
With none or little praise,
But when you rightly organize,
The flag of truce you'll raise.

Our history is not finished quite,
We'll give thousands of verses more,
Connected with the spirit-land,
Pen'd from that lovely shore.

When we've described your rolling orb,
Telling its changes through ;
Then we'll describe the spirit-land,
Telling its changes too.

Mankind was born on earth to die,
The body, not the soul ;
But the spirit can return to earth,
And other forms control.

CPSIA information can be obtained
at www.ICGtesting.com
Printed in the USA
BVHW091737021118
531990BV00019B/1032/P

9 781332 175309